LANDMARK COLLECTOR'S LIBF

THE SPIRIT
BEAUMARIS

ALISON LLOYD-ROBERTS

Hen Blas, the original 15th century
home of the Bulkeley family.
The Market Square is situated on the site

Above: Fryars, home of the Burton Family. Mr. Robert John Jones is leading the horse

Opposite: H.M. The Queen on her visit in 2002
(with Cllr. R.L.Owen, Chairman of Anglesey County Council)

THE SPIRIT OF
BEAUMARIS

THE 20TH CENTURY IN PHOTOGRAPHS

ALISON LLOYD-ROBERTS

Landmark Publishing

Published by

Landmark Publishing Ltd
Ashbourne Hall Cokayne Ave,
Ashbourne Derbyshire DE6 1EJ England
Tel: (01335) 347349 Fax: (01335) 347303
E-mail:landmark@clara.net
Web:www.landmarkpublishing.co.uk

ISBN 13: 978-1-84306-228-8
ISBN 10: 1-84306-228-3

Print: Cromwell Press Ltd, Trowbridge
Design by: Deb Gilling

Front cover: Beaumaris Castle Christmas scene

Back cover (top): West End from Tros-yr-Afon

Back cover (bottom): H.M. The Queen on her visit in 2002

CONTENTS

INTRODUCTION

I have had many years of close connection with the town.
It culminated in my election to the Town Council and eventually
becoming the Town Mayor in 1986. Over the years I have learnt how
special the people of Beaumaris are and many have assisted me in
compiling this collection of photographs.

The images portray life and people in the town, chiefly in the
20th century, on good days and bad; days of enjoyment and those of
quiet reflection. A few photographs are older and include one of the
castle taken in 1864.

I do hope that you enjoy this eclectic collection and that it brings back
other (hopefully happy) memories of times gone by.

Alison Lloyd-Roberts
Colwyn Bay 2006

Landmark welcome proposals for local books of towns and villages

ACKNOWLEDGEMENTS

The author would like to thank the following:
Mrs. Pat Aitken and Mrs. A. Brimecombe, Directors Bulkeley Hotel; Mrs. Pat Caddock;
Mrs. Karen Cross; Mrs. Buddug Davies; Mrs. Isabelle Dixon; Mrs. Marjorie Francis; Mr. 'Patch' Glover;
Mr. John Griffith; Mr. J. Wyn Jones – (Cae Mair); Mr. J.P.; Mr. J.R. Joyce; Mrs. Sheila Jones;
Mr. and Mrs. David Parry; Mr. Tom A. Lewis; Dr. Gwen Richards; RNLI (Mr. John Broughton);
Mrs. Iris Stone; Mr. and Mrs. John Stops; Mrs. Barbara Thomas MBE.
Information on the lifeboats is from *RNLI Motor Lifeboats*, N. Leach, 2005,
also published by Landmark Publishing Ltd

1 STREET AND OTHER SCENES

Castle Street in 1912 with J.R.Jones,
printers and stationers on the left.
The castle gates are just visible
at the end of the street

A later view in Castle Street
with fewer people standing about

Top: John Jones's butchers shop, later the Victoria Stores.
On the right is Girling's fish shop, later Frank & Josephine Hughes (née Girling)
traded from here. See also p.18 (bottom)
Below: Flooding in Castle Street in 1957, due to the castle moat flooding

The pharmacy at 40, Castle Street together with a bill from the shop.

J.P.JOYCE 40 Castle Street, Tel. 810312
BEAUMARIS Anglesey, Gwynedd

Pharmaceutical Chemist and Photographic Dealer

M..

....

....

.................................19........

DEVELOPING
&
PRINTING

Geary & Co, family grocers, of Church Street, now the Bold Arms

Cobbled sets in Church Street. The photograph is of the town's carnival

Top: Street entertainers outside the United Stores in Castle Street run by Mr. Hughes.
His signs advertise Gilbey's wines, Mazawattee tea and Cadbury's cocoa
Bottom: Flooding from the castle moat

Renovation of the Liverpool Arms

Firemen direct water onto a fire at the rear of the Liverpool Arms

Top: More flooding, this time at West End
Bottom: Rough seas at West End, creating more havoc on the road

Cottages in Wexham Street (more recent above)

Upper Wexham Street

A Bill from the Bulkeley Arms Hotel, from 1870. It reads 'Caige to Penmon & back with Lifeboat Crew 6s; Driver 2s'

Bill from the Williams-Bulkeley Arms Hotel, from 1882 for spirits, carriage & telegrams

West End from Tros-yr-Afon, showing the small bridge (foreground)

West End, showing the southwards view

Margaret Street in the 1930s

John Jones's butcher's shop. On the first floor was Mrs. Jones' china shop.
The premises were later the Victoria Stores and is now a delicatessen (see also p.8 top)
Note the phone number: 49!

The North West Venturers Club House at Gallows Point, 1971

The Community Centre (formerly the school caretaker's house) with adjoining Memorial Hall

Situated opposite the castle are the old Ferryman's cottages, seen here after renovation.
The garden is sponsored by *2nd Thoughts*

Coronation street party
at Bryn Teg, 1953

The 2002 Beaumaris Festival

A lovely view of Henllys Hall, formerly the home of the Dwyer-Hampton family,
which later became a monastery, then a hotel and is now apartments

2 SOCIAL EVENTS

The carnival has been a popular event in the annual calendar of Beaumaris. Here are two views from the 1950s. Top: Queen Marjorie (née Shipperlee); Bottom: Queen Ann Oliver Davies (née Williams), the Coronation Year Queen. Both ladies are shown with their 'Court'

Two more Carnival Queens:
Top: Queen Barbara (née Berrisford) Gallichian in 1952;
Bottom: Queen Betty (née Mathews)

The May Queen: Gwyneth (née Jones) above and Christine Jones (née Williams), below

An early Carnival float (top) with an early car festooned for the occasion (bottom)

British Legion Queen Enfys (née Williams) Roberts, with Teresa Lewis, in 1953

Dedication of the War Memorial, 1920

Maypole dancers at the Church fête, probably in Edwardian times

Top: Another group of maypole dancers at the castle
Bottom: Sandra Foden (née Acton) portrays a Council House
and Peter Acton a cowboy, 1950s

The Beaumaris Coronets parading through the town

Morris dancers, 1954

The programme of festivities for the Festival of Britain

23rd AUGUST : THURSDAY
24th AUGUST : FRIDAY

Pageant Play

in the

Castle Courtyard

* * *

We hope to present a short Pageant Play in the historic Courtyard of Beaumaris Castle during the Festival of Britain 'Castle Week'

* * *

Details of this production will be announced in the Press and by Posters at a later date

23.

Advance notice of a Pageant Play to be held in the Castle Courtyard
during the Festival of Britain 'Castle Week', 1951

Militia at Kingsbridge Camp, Llanfaes. It closed in 1920

A view in the sick bay

Top: Beaumaris Women's Institute 40th anniversary
Bottom: Commemorating the World Heritage status of the castle in 1987,
with Sir Richard & Capt., R. Williams Bulkeley

3 THE MENAI STRAITS

The pier in Edwardian times

View from the bay towards West End

The St. Trillo
which plied between
Menai Bridge
and Llandudno

The St. Seiriol
passing Beaumaris Pier
on the way to
Liverpool

Another former old
friend, the St. Tudno,
also on the way
to Liverpool

Stormy weather at the pier. Eventually, the extension with its pavilion
relented to attack by the sea and became unsafe, being demolished half a century ago

A victim of bad weather

Two unusual views of snow on the shoreline

An advert for Saunders Roe former boat builders and bus manufacturers

The original lifeboat, based at Penmon, prior to 1914, when a motor lifeboat was introduced at Fryars Bay. The latter, the *Frederick Kitchen* was from a legacy by Mr. F Kitchen of Caernarfon, costing £3,727.00 and in service from 1914-1945

The lifeboat crew with Coxswain, Hugh Jones. The boat is *Field Marshal and Mrs Smuts*, in service from 1945-1977. She cost £13,865 and weighed 20 tons and was replaced by *Gtr. London II*, which remained here until 1989. The latter had previously been at Southend and had cost £32,163

Award of the RNLI long service medal in 1987. Left to right: David Gallichian; David W. Jones;
Late Col. Cooper; Mike Witkowski; Mayor Cllr. A. Lloyd Roberts; Cllr. Stan Zalot;
David Gallichian had previously been awarded the RNLI Bronze Medal

The RNLI crew receiving the Freedom of the Town

Commemoration
of the 175th
anniversary of
the RNLI

The launch of the rigid-inflatable inshore rescue boat *Blue Peter II* from the new boathouse.
She came into service in September 2000 and remains on station

A lovely photograph of two 'old salts' having a chat on the pier

4 THE CASTLE

For many years, the courtyard walls were bedecked with ivy. Fortunately, it has all been removed

An early view of the castle

The Castle Courtyard when used for tennis

The castle in 1864

A pageant at the castle

An old view from the Castle Meadow

H.M. The Queen visiting the castle in 1958.
She is with the Lord Lieutenant and the Mayor, the late Cllr. William Morris

Below and opposite: Jousting, and summer entertainment at the castle

The original castle gates at the end of Castle Street (above).
The view from Happy Valley (below)

Another view
from Happy Valley,
showing the north side

The castle today,
with swans

Henllys Lane provides
a dramatic background
for the castle, against
The Straits and mountains

5 CHURCHES, CHAPELS AND CHOIRS

The exterior of St. Mary & St. Nicholas's Church from an old postcard (above)
and the nave, taken in the 1950s (below)

Songs of Praise, filmed by the BBC from the Parish Church in 1977. This is a photograph of a TV screen at the time it was broadcast!

Clergy participating in the Beating of the Bounds ceremony.
A service is held en-route at the War Memorial, conducted by the Bishop of Bangor,
Rt. Rev. G.O. Williams, with clergy

The interior of Capel Drindod, Mayor's Sunday Service with Cllr. J.W. Jones, of Caemair, 1991

The service at the opening of the RNLI's new boathouse,
by the late Right Rev., G.O. Williams, Lord Bishop of Bangor

English Presbyterian Church
Beaumaris

Centenary
1870 - 1970

The English Presbyterian Church was situated on the corner of Margaret Street and Church Street.
It is now the Chapel Court flats. This leaflet commemorates its centenary as a chapel in 1970

The interior of the English Presbyterian Church at harvest time

The above church during its redevelopment to Chapel Court

Chapel Court with Wally Hughes cleaning the Post Office windows

CONSECRATION

Of the New Portion of

Beaumaris Cemetery

By The Right Reverend

The Lord Bishop of Bangor

SUNDAY, 7TH OCTOBER, 1951

AT 3 O'CLOCK P.M.

Jarvis & Foster, Printers, Bangor

Order of Service for the consecration of the cemetery extension, 1951

Llaniestyn Church at the 1920 Beating of the Bounds, held every seven years

The Beating of the Bounds, led by the clergy and choir, in the 1960s

Mary, Queen of Martyrs Roman Catholic Church in Rating Row

Beaumaris Choir at Anglesey Chair Eisteddfod 1911

The Saunders Roe Choir, in the 1950s

Rating Row, side view of Mary, Queen of Martyrs Church

6 CIVIC EVENTS

The Beaumaris Silver Band, used at many civic events

The last Assize Service in Beaumaris

The Mayor, Cllr., George Dixon at the reopening ceremony of the Pier, in 1963.
Unfortunately, the image is a little out of focus

The annual Mayor's Parade

Social gatherings form an important part of Civic life

Mayor Alison Lloyd-Roberts receives the 'keys' to Boeing 757 Beaumaris Castle G–BMRA. Left to right: Town Clerk, Bill Hughes; Boeing (Seattle) rep., Bob Hammer; Mr. & Mrs. Lewis and Keith Best, then MP Ynys Môn

The official party aside the new B A Boeing 757.
It is now in service with Easy Jet, but is no longer named Beaumaris Castle

Alison Lloyd-Roberts performing her last engagement as Mayor,
presenting a cheque to Dr. Jim Davies (Co-ordinator of Gwynedd Hospital),
with Claire and Kate Byers

The town's Mayor, Cllr., George Dixon (on the left) greets visitors,
the Mayor & Mayoress of Cardiff in 1963

The Royal Welch Fusiliers on their Freedom March through the town

The Royal Welch mascot leads the Freedom March

Mayor's Sunday 1991, leaving Capel-y-drindod.
Mayor Cllr., JohnWyn Jones (Cae Mair); Mayoress Mrs Nan Jones; Mace Bearer Mr Eirwyn Roberts.
Chapel featured is old Annibynwyr, now Elizabeth Bradley Designs

Borough of Beaumaris

The Beaumaris Coronation Souvenir programme for events at the time of the Queen's Coronation

This is to certify that

Beaumaris

Is a member of the

Walled Towns Friendship

Circle

10th March 2002
Date

John Price

President

Secretary General

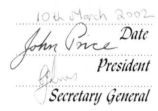

In 2002, the town became a member of the walled town Friendship Circle

The 1986/87 Mayor, Alison Lloyd-Roberts, climbs over the roof of the Dairy at Cefn Farm
during the Beating of the Bounds Ceremony. Half of the roof is in Beaumaris, the other in Llandegfan

The Mayor's regalia, which unusually includes two maces, donated by the Sloan family in 1937.
The two maces may be seen in use overleaf

Cllr. Trevor Roberts & Mrs. Mair Roberts, Mayor & Mayoress, 1969

Mayor's Civic Sunday.
Cllr. Miss M. Conwy Burton

Cllr. Emily Griffith and Mr. J. Griffith. She made history by being made an Alderman of Beaumaris Borough for four days in 1974, whereupon, the town lost its borough status

A photograph of three Aldermen of the former Borough:
Miss Mary Conwy Burton; J. Hugh Thomas OBE; and Major F.L. Arnold (at the rear)

7 TOWN EVENTS

Two views recording the visit of H.M. The Queen in 2002

Queen Alison at the Carnival in 1960 with left to right: Gladwyn Cross; Judy Ward;
Linda Jones; Janice Ward; Irene Powaza; Elspeth (née Williams)

Guides on parade in Church Street

Members of the T.S. *Indefatigable* outside the castle

The day a Spitfire crashed into the home of Mr & Mrs Parry,
and a house in New Street, next door to Gwalia Stores, 1940

Two scenes showing the WI ladies at their proceedings

Preparing refreshments during the Beating of the Bounds procession.
This is an ancient tradition of walking the parish boundary. It maintained continuity, passing
knowledge of its delineation before the days of maps and hopefully preventing disputes in the process

The opening of the new Band Hall in 1987 by Lord Cledwyn of Penrhos

A concert party, with a rendition of Call'R Herring

The Beaumaris Band in 1951, under the leadership of Mr Joe Clayton

Beau the guide dog

In order to raise money for Beau, three 'convicts' were 'tried' and sentenced to
one night each in Beaumaris Jail! Here they are presenting their cheque.
The convicts were Dennis & Tommy Walters and David Jones

Top: Beaumaris British Legion A.G.M. 1950s.
The legion's building is no longer in existence, having been demolished
Bottom: Franciscan Order at Henllys, 1951.
The monastery was later sold and converted into Henllys Hall Hotel

A day trip for the town's Ladies Choir. Back row: Joe Clayton; Peggy Clayton; Mrs. Thomas;
Miss. Thomas; Mrs. W ?; Mrs. Edwards; Mrs. Gallichian; Mrs. H. Hughes; Mrs. Lizzie Owen;
Mrs. Parry; Mrs. Salter; ? ; Mr. R Pritchard. Middle row: Rhona Thomas; Mrs. Mair Jones;
Hazel ?; Mrs. Morris Jones; Ceridwen Jones; Nancy Price; Margaret Jones; Mrs. White.
Front row: Mary Matthews; Mrs. Edith Jones; Mrs. Roberts; Catherine Hughes; Shirley Lewis

Corrine Lindey's Ballet Class Concert, in the 1950s

St. Mary's Church nativity play

Sir Jimmy Saville and Lady Anglesey starting a sponsored walk to raise funds for the RNLI

Taking part in the 2002 Beaumaris Festival

A street party in Rating Row, 2002, to commemorate the Queen's Jubilee

The Brownies in 1958 and more recently

Rememberance Day at the War Memorial

Brownies on parade

The Guides enjoying a bell-ringing session

A Saunders Roe outing

8 SCHOOLS

The Grammar School with Mrs. Madoc Jones and her dog in the foreground.
The school was founded in 1603 by David Hughes

Pupils of the Grammar School. The year is not known

Above: Mr William Bacon with the
Grammar School choir and band

The view from the castle
showing the former
Grammar School and
in particular, Form 3.
The building is now
the library

The former badge of the
County Primary School

View of th town's library
from the castle walls,
formerly Form 3 class rooms

9 POSTCRIPT

Mr. Ted Parry (left); Gerry Sutton (evacuée) and Lawrence Owen (right)
at Liverpool Docks. Gerry was emigrating to Australia

Mr. Rice Parry (painter/decorator)